INTRODUCTION

Well I can't believe how well 'A BAG OF NAILS 1' took off...I feel proper posh now cos on Amazon I'm considered an 'Author' ...wow ...I'm proud of myself...although I wish Tom could have been here with me to share my 3 minutes of fame .. I was overcome by all the well wishes from old friends and new....Most of you - I'd say 90% enjoyed the book and said it brought back good memories from their past...the other 10% didn't 'feel the love' lolol...and did a little bit of raining on my parade..but hey ho it's all good...and it was MY story so I told it MY way !

What I really want this book to be portrayed as – is similar to having a chat or a catch up and a brew with an old friend, remembering our past days and enjoying re-living some of the times through it, I've included amongst my stories pictures of friends, club memorabilia, T.V shows and the toys we would play with – I hope it works for you!

I enjoyed writing the book, and spent most of the time in between writing it and editing it, reminiscing over the events and stuff what had happened all those years ago -

Thing was by the time the first book was published, I realised I'd missed out so many other friends and acquaintances, so many other happenings and stories to tell..there was only one thing for it.....'A BAG OF NAILS 2' FOR OLD TIMES SAKE' ...It had to be done – even more so when quite a lot of you either texted me or stopped me in the street to ask, when or if I would be writing book Number 2..

Although I've still got plenty of tales to tell – I was concerned as to whether there would be enough stories to fill a book ??....The answer was pretty obvious to me – a 'MEMORY SHARE'...bit like one of them time share things but without having to travel abroad for the benefits – So I asked some of my closest friends to share some of their memories with me – and remember fair exchange is no robbery lol xx – I've also decided to include some photos, most of the people in them are real characters in my book. (1 & 2). If you read my first book I explained about my reason for the title 'A BAG OF NAILS' and so for the benefit of those who didn't have the pleasure (lol) of reading my first book, here's why :- Each nail in the bag is compared to the many people i have met and shared, and still share my life with, Imagine a bag of nails, all lengths and sizes, some big and strong holding together heavy structures, some rusty and bent, some small but handy to have around in emergencies ,Some past their use and thrown away, Some not trusted to hold anything together, Some nailed together to construct a formation and still holding it together after many years. Some lost forever or used in new formations or elements, I hope you can understand and compare similarity to this with people you have met throughout your life. I believe everyone has their own 'bag of nails'

I hope you enjoy reading about some of mine..x

The stories in this book are as true to my knowledge as I remember, some of the events are in the 70's, 80's & also 90's now, though still worth remembering, some tweeks have been made here and there to save embarrassment, and to avoid any 'jobsworths' wanting to once again 'try' to rain on my parade – something I'm now long past worrying about lol.

I never regret anything I say, cos if I didn't

want to say it – I would have kept my mouth

shut in the first place !

So this book is a mish mash of bits n bobs from here and there, still true stories, but with some added interruptions of memory joggers from our past – I've even added quite a lot of pics, and although we are a little older, everyone still recognisable just .....

FOR OLD TIMES SAKE.....

THE PUBS

Farnworth years ago had an abundance of pubs..always packed to the brim, music, brawls, card games, - always laughs.

THE BLACKHORSE

The Blackhorse at the top of Market Street is one of the few pubs still open, usually busy and now boasts some great Northern soul nights – complimentary of a good friend of mine D.J Bernard Pearson, and old blue eyes himself Gary Roscoe another Northern soul buff...

It was, few years ago managed by two more good friends of mine Mickey and Elaine Waters, sadly Mick passed away, a lovely guy but Im sure will be remembered by many. I remember my early teens playing kiss catch and dodge ball on Pilky Park with Mick, with Kath Alker, the Raynor brothers and Graham Shuck, I was a little tub then and couldn't run for toffee, but still they never seemed to catch me ???? - lol.

Jimmy Reynor had a bright orange 'bond buggy' a tiny 3 wheeled car what lifted up from the front bonnet so you could get in, loved it when he gave me a spin round the park in it...

The Blackhorse was the main pub we all used to congregate in years ago when we had the 'never to be forgotten' power cuts – the tables would be donned with large white candles and we'd all sit round in the golden glow telling ghost stories, jokes and making a general nuisance of ourselves, but it was bloody good fun. Hassy – Philip Haslam and his buddy Graham Marsh were the perfect entertainers on these nights, keeping us all amused with their gags, two genuinely funny guys, who both could impersonate certain celebrities to perfection – well we thought they could lol.

At one point Hassy and Graham – or 'Plum' as we called him concocted a brilliant double act and performed it in several Farnworth pubs – just for the hell of it – The one that sticks in my mind was their take off, of a chart hit at the time 'Whispering grass' Plum kitted out in the Sergeant's uniform as Windsor Davies, and Hassy kitted out in his Jungle Safari suit as Don Estelle..Brilliant !!

what I'd give to see it again...

THE BLACKHORSE

YE OLD THREE CROWNS

YE OLD THREE CROWNS, also known as 'Smokeys' another pub still rearing its head above the water, was then inhabited with the older couples and 'Tap roomers' - workers who would call in for a pint after their shifts had finished.

Nowadays owned by another friend Paul Riley 'Polly' (one of my past dart's rivals who never really accepted the fact that I beat him at dart's .....several times lol).

Smokey's now houses a good selection of mixed ages, reasonable prices for the beer and keeps the punters happy, with a large heated smoking area and good music. (wow I sound like an estate agent lolol)

YE OLDE THREE CROWNS –
SMOKEYS

Crossing over the road on Market street
we have .....

THE POST OFFICE

This, years ago was the watering hole of
the likes of Arney Brown, Albert
Howarth, Jimmy Murphy, Johnny Heinz,
Danny McVeigh, Tommy Belk, Mel
Fleming, Jimmy Evans, Joe and Billy
Deveney, - all notably 'hard men'
nerves of steel, they didn't give a fuck
who you were just as long as you knew
your place.

Most punters did – but the odd few who
slipped the net usually spent a night or
two in Bolton Royal...

Nowadays, run by yes – another couple
of friends of mine (why do I have so

many friends in the pub trade ?? lol) Tim Whinchup and Ellen Mc Evans. It's now a little haven for regulars who enjoy the 'Monday' club and also throws a good few charity nights – enjoyed by all.

 Frequented by 2 of Farnworths funniest characters, Pablo and Phil Townsend – 'Towny – who are always ready for a laugh and who both have this immense passion for 'dressing up'

...and they certainly go to town when they do pantomime dames, pirates, garden elves, show girls whatever takes their fancy....lol.

THE POST OFFICE

THE QUEENS

Just a little further down the road we had the 'Queens ' , this was then like the 'sister' pub to the 'Post office' serving the same punters, except on Friday nights which was 'disco night' then it was anything goes, we had Shaun Broadhurst from Little Hulton – The proud Lambretta riding skinhead resident D.J – top lad, although was a little partial to a bit of 'bovver' every now and then.

A good friend of my Hubby's Tom.

Later on in years the pub was run by Thomas and Diane Jackson.

The Queens was sadly pulled down several years ago and has now been rebuilt as a Plumbers merchants, and sells taps for baths instead of taps of beer!

THE QUEENS

THE MARKET INN

Readers of my first book might recall
that was where our 'lot' would spend
most of our time. If the walls in that pub
could speak – ohhhh what stories it
could tell. It was the 'hub' of our
lifestyle, anything that went on in
Farnworth – The Market Inn would
always be the first to know who ,what,
where, or when! The nights of 'AT'
drinking spent there, the arsenal of
things I shouldn't be writing about
hidden there, the neighbouring town
battles, The pharmaceutical transactions
that took place, The haven for fugitives,
it was the original 'hole in the wall'....but
it was our 'hole in the wall' and the
volume of loyalty, trust and friendship
we all shared will never be forgotten.

THE MARKET INN

Crossing over from the Market Inn
through what used to be the Market
Stalls (also sadly now gone to a Market
stall heaven) we head for...

THE SADDLE

This is now today just a small patch of
land decorated with concrete barrels
barring the entrance site for travellers
and gypsies. The Saddle one of the
most frequented pubs of all the
'Farnworth Lot' mainly the elders, Jimmy
Kelly, Mick Walsh – Wally, Mick Hughes,
Jimmy Rothwell (although he was from
little Hulton), Paul & Harry Worthington,
Paul Topping – Topsy, Phil Townsend –
Towny, Brian Howarth (he moved to
Blackpool) Jack Cartwright, Brian
Goddard, Jimmy Harrison, Dave Whittle
– Pollywick, Ferdy, Tetley, Paul, &
Howard Wilky, Tony Walton, Frank
Powery, Billy & Roy Isherwood, Les
Robinson, Mel Fleming, Tony Cunliffe,
Steve Barber, John Beret – braces,
David & Brian Tickle, Skizz (and his

fucking car air horn well that's how we all described it !)) Cyril Lindley, Carl Baxter, Ste & Billy Lane...Stephen Whittlestone (who is now living the dream in the U.S.A) and probably a shed load more I've forgotten..It's here on Saturday night when most of our lot were ready for Wigan Casino, this lot would meet up in their two-tone pants, penny round shirts and highly polished loafers, then make their way to Moor Lane Bus station and a 'free' bus would drive straight through to Blackpool Mecca. They'd return home next morning on that same free bus, completely wrecked after having the best night ever.

THE SADDLE

Across the street from the Saddle, was
and still is ..

THE BRITTANIA – THE BRITT

Unbelievably another pub that's still survived the ghost town curse and nowadays one of the most frequented pubs in Farnworth.

In the 70's & 80's the Britt was pretty run down, white net curtains turned yellow from years of park drive and capstan full strength smoke, the carpets so worn they were more acceptable as lino, majority of punters were local elderly piss heads or wino's, walking in the tap room was like walking back in time – to London's foggy nights, jugs of ale, and big bosomed bar staff, thick with smoke, half expecting Jack the Ripper to pop his groomed head round the lounge room door, or Sweeney Todd and his Mrs, sharpening their cut throat razors waiting for their next pie filling.

Nowadays, a decent little pub, meeting place for all ages – and no London Fog!

THE BRITTANIA

THE FREEMASONS

When I was at school, my friend Julie
Jackson, lived here, I had a few sleep
overs there when I was a kid. I thought
it was a mansion.

I lived in a small terraced off-license with
my parents, she lived in this massive
pub with what seemed like hundreds of
rooms, it was great.

Over the years long after Julie and her
family had left, the pub became similar
to the Britt, needed a good doing over,
not many of our lot ventured in here, so
theres nothing much to say about it.
However years have passed, times
have changed and now it's been tidied
up a bit and gets the older punters doing
there afternoon half a lager sessions,
and the younger 'occasional' knob head

'I think I'm ten men' evening drinkers

who are monitored by the burly

doormen. Well at

Least it's still standing !

THE FREEMASONS

THE WELLINGTON

....another of 'our lots' regular drinking spots, here they had a big piano, and me and my mates Viv and Helen would spend many a drunken night singing away – making our own words up to anything the local self appointed barley wine drinking pianist Ronnie (a bloody good pianist though) would rattle out. I remember one night in there with my pals Col and Nelly, three girls came in from the side entrance, One of them had been seeing Cols fella behind her back, us three stood at the other side of the open bar in the other room, the three wannabe neverbees stood there with a challenging smile across their big ugly rimmel caked faces. Without one word spoken, all three of us (me, Nelly and Col) lifted our tonic bottles a lobbed them right across at the strumpets – then all hell broke loose – it was like a scene from Armageddon, don't know how or why but all the pub erupted everyone was fighting with everyone, even the bloody landlord and landlady. Well it's enough to say the dibble was called and after a ride around in a panda car for an hour and a good bollocking we were let off with a warning. Classy birds us!

THE WELLINGTON PUB

the
wellington pub

drink . music . sports
relax . enjoy

www.thewellypub.co.uk

FREEHOUSE
OPENING TIMES

THE VICTORIA or the 'VIC'

Another pub that has bit the dust and no longer exists. This too was another pub I can't really comment on for the 70's & 80's as I think I only went in once – and then it was for some change for a fiver for the bus.

However over the years it became quite a popular little refreshment palace, and run by Jennifer became popular at the weekends with the karaoke and fun themed nights, we called it handbags, haven't a clue where we got that from ?? but handbags then progressed to 'flying handbags' and I still haven't a clue why ?

THE VICTORIA – FLYING HANDBAGS

THE ROSE & CROWN

Also known as 'Scarletts' and 'RAC'.

One night in here the Farnworth lads were having a beer, Calm and collected yet Intruding on their territory in came a dozen Little Hultoners, and once again yet another scene from Armageddon, there were lead bars, knives, baseball bats, and bottles all being brandished, thrown, and bashed about each other's bodies, every single window had a bar stool put through and ended up in the middle of the road on Market street.

I remember seeing a woman coming out of the Freemasons and picking up a couple of the stools and running like a sewer rat back into the Freemasons pub hoping no-one had seen her.

Police sirens alerted everyone to do a runner, our lot went to the only safe house – The Market Inn.

Sat in the Market, all calm and listening to the Stylistics, 'You make me feel brand new' - in walks Mr C.I.D himself, sergeant Clugstone and one of his wing men.

'Right you little bastards - Tommy, Robbie Eeky, Megs, Bren, Marley get your fucking arses outside your all nicked' he snarled - Mr C.I.D knew everybody by their first names

– he loved being a copper! Outside the lads were all denying any knowledge of the trouble at the Rose & Crown sworn they'd been in the 'Market' all night!...along came the reinforcements - The black Mariah and out popped some more boys in blue, truncheons in hands......Tommy was the main target and I remember one of the new copper cadets – trying to make his mark – directing his commands and his truncheon threateningly, at Tommy – big mistake!!

Tommy whipped the truncheon out of his hand and smacked him across his head with it – The copper was gobsmacked, the melee then was like a scene from the Laurel and hardy era of the keystone cops...looking back now it was soooo bloody funny – our lads were all over the coppers – hadn't got a clue what had hit them, however the long arm of the law managed to cuff Tommy and Mick and fling them into the back of the Mariah....

Me ??? well I was like a rabid banshee and proceeded to jump on the back of the rookie cop, legs all astraddle, very unladylike – I was flung onto the bonnet of a parked taxi and threatened with a night in the cells. Didn't happen though

THE ROSE & CROWN

One of the main social clubs in Farnworth was..

THE VETS

Don't think anybody in Farnworth has NEVER been in here...It was the hub for all Weddings, Christenings, 21st, 18th Birthdays, any celebration that was worth going to was held at The Vets..

The closing of the Vets a couple of years ago was a sad event, so many memories for so many people – now its a Dental surgery – all appointmenst are at 2.30 (tooth hurtee) sorry its an old one I know – but I had to put it in lol...

The Vets had some amazing nights there, live bands and singers, bingo for grandma, every New year they laid a spread on for its members..Roy Burton was the resident landlord, loved by many and still knocking about in Farnworth, always ready for a chat, I can honestly say in all the time I've known Roy – he's always got a smile or a friendly word for everyone.

I was lucky enough to have my 40th Birthday party there (just a few years ago lol) and can honestly say its a night I will never forget, there was over 450 guests, I remember Roy Burton worrying about seats and tables, but we all managed.

There were friends come from Australia, America, South Africa, Scotland, Jamaica - It was absolutely brilliant – a night I will never forget! Ive still got all my Birthday cards from then – 239 to be exact , I treasure every single one of them!

My daughter decided to hire a stip-o-gram for the 'do' well he came in dressed as a nun, and then stripped off to a tarzan loin cloth, to reveal a round chubby man who was also an absolutely brilliant comedian, and it made my night.

FARNWORTH OLD VETERANS CLUB

THE CHURCH HOTEL

Just slightly off the beaten track and halfway down Church Road, we have last but not least, The Church Hotel. Years ago it was a quiet little haven where couples could go and have a quiet drink and listen to the dated jukebox.

Later on it was taken over by Vic Magari, and Pat Stanley, Ive spent many a new year there and had a brilliant time.

I remember one new year going in I was wearing a long black velvet strappy dress, I thought I looked brill lol...the dress had a slit up to the knee, My legs where as white as the pure driven snow to be on the safe side I coloured my legs with deep brown fake tan – just above my knee.   Towards midnight I was going to start the 'Aulld lang syne' song on the Karaoke, I went to the loo first, coming back into the large filled lounge I felt pretty good as I realised I was getting a few wolf whistles, beaming smile on my face and thinking I was the bomb lol...I reached for the microphone.

Tom grabbed my arm and said 'Sort your dress out love' for a few seconds I realised the wolf whistles and the smiling faces wasn't because I was going to belt out a 'Robbie Burns' number it was because after leaving the loo, all the back of my long dress was firmly tucked into the back of my 'very large' white panty girdle, my two tone flabby half brown half snow white legs wobbled like a savage blancmange –

Now I had a face like a wasp sucking on a Mexican chilli ! so embarrassed – but like the good trouper I am, the show must go on – ha ha ha.

I saw the funny side along with about 60 others and sang Auld Lang Syne, everyone was in hysterics !

Don't think I've ever sung that song since..

Nowadays the Church Hotel caters for the more younger end and is run by Pat, and her four children, and is still going strong!

There were many more pubs in the centre, now all gone to the big brewery graveyard – Clock Face, Wagon & Horses (Blackjacks), Horseshoe, Bowling Green, Travellers Rest, Ellesmere, Bird in t' Hand.

Think everyone of us has got a memory from one or two of these watering holes, what we can look on and smile about.

THE CHURCH HOTEL

ST.GREGORYS CLUB – THE PHOENIX CLUB

St. Gregorys social club wasn't one of our venues in the 70's & 80's, it was more for the Stalwart catholic congregation, and their families, however I think it's worth a mention as most of us remember in the 2000 – 2001 years, it was the base for 'Peters Kay's 'Phoenix Nights'.

I was on the committee there, and was lucky enough to be one of the extras on the shows, as was my husband Tommy (He was the gypsy king with the brown fringed jacket) and my son, Jonathan and daughter, Sherri-Lee, we had some great fun there filming, and met some of the stars involved, some were nice – some weren't ! – One of the nicest guys on the show was Dave Spikey who

48

played Jerry St.Clair, we'd have a drink in the lounge with him some nights after filming, no airs or graces a genuine nice bloke.   Peter Kay was a nice enough bloke – a genuinely funny man but he took his work seriously, which resulted in a great comedy series.

When it was my son's 18th Birthday (during filming) Peter gave him a very large bottle of Scotch Whiskey and a signed framed picture of himself signing 'Have It Jono!!!' on the bottom, - We've still got that picture hung on the wall in what was then, Jonathans bedroom.

Nowadays reverted back to St.Gregory's club, It's a large venue for Weddings, Christenings, Birthdays etc..

ST.GREGORYS SOCIAL CLUB

THE PHOENIX CLUB

SHOPS & CAFES

Farnworth could at one time boast a brilliant Market, loads of different stalls loads of different characters, Ali an Indian man used to have the tights and knicker stall, Bryn would always have black bin bags of coats, the women would all grab the bags as he unloaded them from his car and root through for their kids anoraks or parka coats for school, before he had time to lay his stall out, resulting in a big heap of coats piled up on the wooden stall.

Even after all these years, Bryn up until this last year still stood the Markets, now I'm thinking he's retired.

There was 'Dad and Lads' in Brackley Street, all the lads got their 'trendy clothes' from there,

Also on Brackley street was The old fashioned 'Toffee Shop', wow the smell that hit you when you walked in, treacle, aniseed, winter nips, cough candy, cherry lips, chewing nuts (which wern't even nuts they were little caramel balls covered in chocolate) sarsparalla drops, pineapple chunks, American cream soda, rainbow crystal kaylie...black jacks, fruit salad chews, Invalid toffee, peppermint chews, Spanish gold (that was sugar coated stringy chewy stuff – made to resemble tobacco – probably get hung drawn and quartered now by health & safety for selling it) I loved them all...

All we have left now of that Market is a large space of derelict land – such a waste.

TOGNARELLI'S

Another meeting place on a Saurday afternoon would be Tognarelli's or 'Togs' a large ice cream parlour on Higher Market Street, here we would swap record singles and read 'The Record song book' a book what came out every fortnight with all the words to the latest chart songs, whilst eating a large bowl of Jimmy Togs smooth vanilla 99 with a Cadburys flake..

In them days it was proper Vanilla ice cream, not todays shitty synthetic rubbish...even the flakes were three times bigger than they are today as well as being 10 times cheaper! – and whilst I mention it – What about Mars bars ??? How small are they today in comparison to how big they used to be ?? one bite and its gone !! Think Cadburys and

Mars should be boycotted until we get the proper size back in the shops !

Not forgetting 'little Jimmy Togs' who used to hike his 'togs' ice cream van round the estates, I remember my Mum used to take a large bowl to him and get it filled for our 'dessert' treat for about 2 shillings (10 pence nowadays).

Some other Saturday afternoons were spent at Spa Road in Bolton...

<u>THE NEVADA</u> – skating rink

Here's where everyone donned the metal roller skates and batted round the rink like Olympic entrants for the 1980's federation of artistic skating skills award.

Saturday evening the rink would be used as a dance floor for literally hundreds, who would 'bop' away to the 'Bay City Rollers' tartan teen sensations from Edinburgh, singing 'Bye Bye Baby or David Bowies 'Starman', Led Zeppelin, Pink Floydd, Queen, Black Sabbath, The Who, The Rolling Stones, and Abba to name a few..

Most of us calling at the 'Chippy' on the way home, bag of chips wrapped in the 'News of the World' smothered in salt and vinegar, now also another memory of the past, obsolete due to health & safety standards !

Sadly the Nevada burned down several years ago.

Talking about chippy's – there used to be a chippy up Highfield Road and you could go in and order a pea wet barm, this consisted of A barmcake cut in two then filled with a large helping of chips, then the pea gravy in the pea pan was spooned over the chips – sometimes we got a pickled onion with it – bloody lovely !

THE NEVADA AFTER FIRE BURNED IT DOWN

BIRCHES PASTY SHOP/CAFE

On the Farnworth bus station arcade – or 'The Warry' as we all called it there was a pasty shop, 'Birches' best pasties ever!! It had a large cafe seating area inside and sometimes some of us would buy a pasty and a couple of orange juices between four of us just to be able to sit in if it was cold, raining or just to sit somewhere.

Most of the staff didn't mind, except for one woman a little round dark haired miserable, scowling, grumpy battleaxe who had a big tuft of hair sprouting from a large pimple on her chin, she absolutely hated me !!

No matter how many times I went in – She always banned me for something !! I think it was because I gave her the nick name 'Bluebeard' and then everyone started to call it her – that woman was so ugly her birth certificate must of been an apology letter from the condom factory !....Never knew what happened to her when Birch's shut down, I'm thinking she got herself a job in an haunted house....

KOH-I-NOOR & JOEY BANGLAS

These two Indian restaurants on Lower Market Street, served the best curries and pappadums everrr!!...

These were the two places we'd go to celebrate birthdays, engagements, weddings etc..I don't think a weekend ever went by without one of the Farnworth lads going in for a curry, then at the last mouthful of chapatti do a runner, with the restaurant staff waving their arms in the air and chasing them down Market Street cursing in their 'Broken English' Indian accent- 'Farnworth bastard boys' !!

The lads would disappear into Farnworth Park – Funny thing was – they would always go back week or two after and get served again!

THE 'WAKES'

Twice a year the fair would come to Farnworth or as we knew it then 'The Wakes'.

The Wakes always had this smell you could identify by a mixture of Hot dogs, burgers, fried onions and candy floss, mixed with a little machinery oil...but it always smelled good!!

I think I remember one of the owners were called Wilox, though I could be wrong, but the Cubbins Fairground people were always on site, The Waltzer was my favourite, mainly because I fancied one of the lads on the ride - Baz Rogers, my first crush, I think all the girls liked him, but I was sure he had only eyes for me – because he gave me a vinyl single – 'Puppy Love' by Donny Osmond...I've still got that single vinyl somewhere in my attic...lol

Some of the other 'fair' lads were Lee Harrop, Danny McVeigh, Chang and Rib, another fair lad I liked was Ronald Cubbins, they used to call him Bridget the Midget, he moved to live in Blackpool last I heard, but that was another record for my collection – Bridget the Midget by Ray Stevens....

Another of the rides which I havn't seen for years was 'The Speedway' this was a large structure similar to the Waltzer what spun round really fast, not a good idea to ride on when you've just had a fill of black peas and hot potatoes from Mr Baxters stall, I recall only too well one Dark Novemeber night after a full tub of Peas and large paper bag of potatoes I stupidly went on the 'Speedway' – A group of Greasers (skinhead rivals) stood around the gallery surrounding the Speedway, as it slowed down I stood up to get off only to completely cover three of the leather clad ruffians from head to foot in black pea vomit, the shock of it stunned them long enough for me to gallop over the barrier and escape – God only knows what my fate would have been if they had got hold of me that night.

THE GOOD, THE BAD, AND THE STUPID or

METAL MICK & KETAMINE KAZ (KAREN)

These two 90's scroats originally came from Breightmet, Mick was a big ugly bloke who apparently had broke his jaw in an accident, part of his jaw was fixed with metal.

Ketamine Karen – well the name speaks for itself, She was a smelly flea infected crack head who didn't give a shit about anything or anybody, they had three small kids, Mick was loud and a bully, he like his special brew and could often be heard bellowing orders to his fleabag, and also them poor little kids.

The children, were all blonde with bright blue eyes – tarnished with fear and neglect, don't think they ever owned a clean vest or T.shirt between them, and they would often be wandering around the estate really late at nights on their own, their parents probably in the pub or smashed out of their faces.

One of these nights, one of the little ones had wandered into an area where there was a big lodge at the back of 'old' St.Gregorys school, the little one couldn't have been more than 5 or 6 years old, the inevitable happened and the child fell in, It was Mid November – bloody cold.

Dont know whether you can call it luck or not, but there was a couple on the lodge doing a bit of 'courting' they heard the child's cries and the guy jumped in and pulled him out, The little boy was in shock and the Police was called, he was taken to Townleys hospital, eventually I don't know how but they found out where he lived and notified his unconcerned parents, who were both unaware the child was missing – even though it had gone 11 o'clock at night.

Karen went to the hospital – and stayed the night – to save her face I suppose.

They both returned home next day, to a house which was eerily quiet, looking around the sink Karen noticed an old tea towel what looked like it had blood stains on it, I'm assuming nothing seemed out of place – as the house was always a mess, but Karen shouted upstairs to Mick. 'I'm up here' he snarled back. Karen walked up the stairs to find Mick lay on the dirty filthy stained mattress, cigarette in one hand and a bottle of Strongbow in the other.

'Where's the kids ?' she asked. ' In their bedroom – the little bastards – They'll know better than to leave Joey (not his real name) on his own again' he said

'Fucking embarrassing the fucking family like that' his words slurred and he took another swig from the bottle.

Karen went into the kids room, It stank of stale pee and dirty laundry, the mattress had been removed from the beds and the two other children were huddled up in a corner of the room

Karen drew back the curtains, they elder boy flinched at the light, his faced swollen and bruised and dried blood ran down the front of his lips from his nose, the other child, his blond hair blood stained from his brothers damaged face, his eye swollen and purple his scruffy top had been ripped open and red marks showed that he had also taken a beating.

Karen turned to leave the room, Mick was right behind her 'Nip to the shop and get me some cigs will you' he demanded. 'I've no money left Mick' Karen replied.

Without any hesitation the evil brute smashed his fist right into the side of Karen's head 'You had a fiver left last night you lying cow! He screamed

'Karen backing herself into the corner of the room knowing full well what to expect ' I used it on the taxi to come home from the hospital' she cried.

Bang!! Again Mick's fist hit into her traumatised skull.

Karen dropped to her knees and covered her head, the three children now all cowering in terror, they had seen this so many times before.

Mick grabbed at Joey picked him up with one hand and kick dropped him like some flyaway football, he too dropped like a lead balloon to the bare floorboards.

'That's your fault you snivelling little bastard, you used my fucking money for your fucking taxi !!!.

The elder of the three children stood up as if wanting to protect his little brother, but soon retreated when he saw the Raging red bulging eyes of his tormentor.

He walked from the room swearing and muttering to himself, but not before landing one hefty kick to Karen's stomach.

'You'd better think pretty quick about finding some cash you slag – Now get your arse up and go find some money for me !! – he shouted back to her 'Or you'll be more than sorry'

Karen got up clutching her stomach and scrambling from the room like a disturbed Rat – not once did she notice the three little mortified waifs clutching on to each other in floods of tears and blind terror!

She ended up at Mo's house, further down her street – as she normally did when she needed money for beer or a 'fix' for herself, she told Mo what had happened, as usual soft hearted Mo, handed over a few quid to Karen hoping it would keep Mick pacified – until the next time!

This time though, Mo was more concerned – the beatings had become more frequent to the children.

Later that day she called round to her sisters and told her the story, Well as it happened Mo's sister was the Mother of one of our lot, the story came out – we all sat in the Market Inn as Martin told us – not one of us spoke throughout, we couldn't believe this cruel monster and his useless arse wipe of a wife hadn't been charged or at least had the children put into care for protection.

Well the dibble wasn't doing much about it !! – One thing about our lads was as much as they could act like hooligans and yobs at times – they hated wife beating or children being physically abused.

Enough said that Tommy, Robbie and Eeky decided to pay Metal Mick and Ketamine Kaz a visit.

There wasn't any big discussion or planning needed they knew what had to be done. The three of them chose the next day to pay their respects.

I can't imagine what Metal Mick thought when he opened his door –

'Alright lads – what can I do for you' he said The lads without any response pushed Mick into his living room and onto the scruffy torn sofa.

He tried to get up, but with one mighty lunge Tommy kicked him back down, once again trying to get up and react to Tommy's kick he was knocked back down this time with a crunch of a punch to the side of his head from Robbie,...and then the party began,

They made sure Mick felt the pain them kids had felt. Stopping for breath the lads heard a noise from upstairs, Eeky went up the stairs and to the bedroom door with a large black bolt fastened on the outside, he unlocked the door and entered.

The room was dark and smelly, the windows were blacked out with an old velvet curtain what had been fastened around the window frame with drawing pins.

Eeky could faintly see in the corner of the room huddled up on a single bare mattress, the three little waifs.

It's alright cock' said Eeky, and he attempted to usher them out from the room, the eldest boy winced as he touched his arm, and once out on the landing Eeky noticed the lad had several cigarette burns on his forearm 'Bastard!' he said and bringing the lads down to the front door.

He Instructed the eldest to go with his brothers down the street to Mo's.

Coming back into the living room he told Tommy and Robbie what he'd just seen.

By now Mick was cowering on the floor hands covering his head and pleading with the lads with pathetic excuses about how he didn't mean to hurt the kids, Robbie went into the kitchen and minutes later returned with a kettle of boiling hot water, instantly pouring it all over Micks crotch –

'Now that's what a proper a fucking Burn feels like mate' he said, Mick's screams could be heard streets away, Yes he got 'banged' like a screen door in a hurricane!

I'm assuming at some point someone must of called an ambulance, the lads didn't stop there long enough to find out who! Mick was left in a broken, bloodied pulp on his living room floor. He'd had a taste of his own medicine.

I know at some point both his hands had been broken, don't know how – and if I did I wouldn't say. He wouldn't be using them again any time in the near future to brutally abuse them little boys, or anyone else for that matter.

All we heard after that was that the Ambulance had taken Mick away.

Mo had eventually called the Social Services the children had at last gone into care.

Crabby Karen left shortly after, we heard she had been moved to somewhere in Liverpool, I hope to god she never had any more kids.

We then learned from Mo, that all three children had been found an home 'together' I hope they had a good life, no one deserved it more than them three little ones.

FAROUK THE FAKIR

Farouk the Fakir or as we knew him Farouk the 'Faker' constantly tried to convince us that he was the son of a Indian Maharaja King, truth was his Dad had a Handbag stall on Pendlebury Market.

He was a decent lad really and just wanted to fit in with our lot, and he'd try so hard especially, on match days when the lads went to Burnden.

In them days there was lots of racism, and some of the more controversial (our lot weren't) skinheads hated any foreigners especially if their skin colour wasn't the colour of a co-ops silver top bottle. This didn't deter Farouk, he'd walk proudly with the lads down Manny Road swearing and shouting at any brown skinned foreigners that crossed their path.

Farouk believed he was white ! 'You wanna a taste of this !' he'd shout at the dumbstruck Asian lads waving his fist.

The puzzled Asians would look at him then back at the lads in disbelief, not being able to register his strange behaviour towards them.

Farouk did everything we thought an Indian lad (or Prince lol) shouldn't have done, he drank like a Fish, he ate Bacon Barms, Popped a few tabs here and there, and constantly ogled pretty blonde girls – he was one on his own.

Farouk was an amazing dancer, and he lived for his 'all nighters' nights at Wigan Casino, The Torch in Stoke and Bolton's Va-Va, never once leaving the dance floor all through the night, and believe me as any Northern souler will tell you – Northern Soul Dancing had a good chance of either leading to immediate resuscitation or a cardiac arrest.

Sadly, his Father passed away and Farouk and the rest of his family moved to live with relatives in London. I sometimes wonder what became of him.

A FEW MEMORY JOLTS FROM SOME
OF THE ALL-NIGHTERS...AND CLUBS

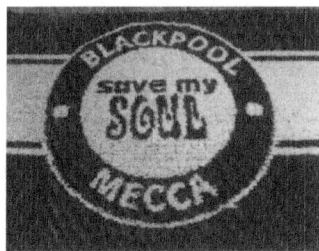

These badges were proudly stitched on our tops, jackets or all-nighter bags.

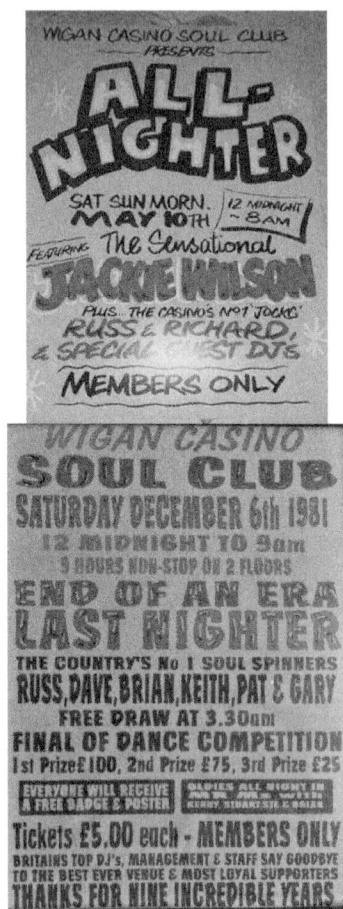

ANGIE

Well I could have mentioned 'Angie' in my 'Bag of Nails' number 1 book, but if I did I couldn't have wrote about her honestly without causing some ill feeling amongst us – because in them days I hated her – and she hated me! With a passion let me tell you, without going into too much detail, we couldn't sit in the same room without kicking off ! Well over the years we've both grown up, married had children and we still freaking hate each other !!! Lol, no, only joking ! we actually get on really well now and have laughed about our past trials and tribulations on several occasions. I speak to her regularly – usually through social media – or on the odd night out.

I've recently spoken to her, and she knows there's a little chapter where I mention her, she was part of our crowd, and I think good or bad memories forge any relationship when you grow up. Over the last couple of years we both lost our husbands, and share a common sadness and loss in our lives, this also has re-enforced our friendship. So enough said.

BILLY BUTLINS - PWHELLI

One summer, me and Tom decided we'd have a go at working the holiday camps, We managed to get jobs at 'Butlins' in Pwhelli, and travelled down one Friday night, ready to start being prepped on the Saturday for our bar work.

The camp looked o.k in the dark when we got there, but when we were led to a more discreet area of the place to the 'staff' living quarters.

We realised we'd come to 'Hell' and half expected the devil himself to appear with his hoofed feet, pronged fork and red horns, to show us the ropes, - what a shit hole!

In the room we shared we had two single iron beds, grubby stained mattresses, and two sofa cushions (not pillows) the room was about 7ft by 7ft square and had a washing line rope strung across with a flimsy, dirty, old hessian type sheet separating the beds.

There was a small sink at the end of the bed – one tap – 'COLD'.

No chairs or cupboards – nothing else! Our spare clothes stayed in our small suitcases, 1 electric socket which we found wasn't even working !

Me and Tom looked at each other and laughed, believe me, not with joy, but with WTF had we got ourselves into here.

Too tired by now to think straight, or 'escape' we tried to get our heads down for the night.

Maybe things might look better in the morning......or maybe not|!

We were woken up next morning around 6 o'clock, with a loud bugle like screech coming from a nearby tannoy – a voice told all new staff to congregate on the small park area nearby – which we did.

There was about ten of us and we were segrated into groups of two and three's, Me and Tommy were allocated to the 'Bier Keller' here we were given our 'uniforms' Tommy was given a white shirt with red & green braces and a green & red trilby hat, which I never saw him wear lol.

My outfit was a short green & red bibbed dress (a bit like you would imagine 'Heidi wore' when she lived in the mountains) white puff sleeved top worn underneath and white knee length socks!

I had to wear my hair in bunches tied with green & red ribbons, which had two f****** bells attached to them – which the manager insisted I wore at all times whilst working behind the bar and whilst serving drinks – God Help me!!!

The bar manager was a small tubby bloke called Barry, with greased back hair and a small moustache – appropriate we thought for the 'German bar'.

He was rude and arrogant and treated the staff like muck, no people skills what so ever, none of the staff liked him.

The Bier Keller was a large room filled with very long table and benches, here punters would sit, stand and dance on the tables after they had filled up on the large 2litre steins of 'German beer'.

There was always one dick head whose wife had nipped to the loo, who decided to get brave and 'try his luck', had more hands going than an octopus.

Then as soon as the Mrs returned he'd conform to his brow beaten, hen pecked comatose state, like nothing had happened.

We had no choice but stay – we hadn't got enough money for our fare home so we had to work the usual two weeks in hand.

Our time there began at 7 a.m, breakfast, then 8.am to the Bier Keller to clean tables and set out mats, clean the glasses, mop the floors etc 12 p.m dinner yum yum a variety of prison slop watery potatoes, mince and cardboard crust pie, and if we managed to get there early enough we managed to get a dessert, sago pudding or jam pie.

This was definitely living the life !! Back to the Beer Keller for 4 p.m sorting the barrels, putting up bunting and balloons for the 7 p.m opening – Teatime was 5 p.m – More slop and then back again to the Beer Keller for 6.30 p.m – Then we were there until the last punter had drunk his last stein which was normally about 1.30 a.m.

We had 2 half days a week off.

We were instructed or 'commanded' to keep a smile on our faces at all times – easy peasy !

On the Friday of the 2nd week, (pay day) we had decided to work our last night, we needed to go home, we were going for the 'great escape' trouble was the part of the camp where we were 'imprisoned' had coiled barbed wire around the 4 metre mesh fencing.

We had no choice but to approach the 'German border guard' Barry and tell him we wanted to leave.

He wasn't a happy man, telling us we had let the camp down and that there was no ready replacements for us.

We were adamant – but Barry still had our wages! For the next 4 -5 hours Barry made our resignation difficult, he inspected our uniforms for damage or stains, we had to fill numerous forms in the 'office' to release us from our jobs and refused us any meals or refreshments before we left saying we no longer were employed there so couldn't use the facilities.

He inspected our bags before we left in case we had stolen any property belonging to Billy Butlin.

Eventually and reluctantly, he give us our pay which was nowhere near the two weeks pay we had earned, and we were escorted out towards a large back entry which housed the rubbish bins from the kitchens.

'I'll go and get these filthy uniforms cleaned now' he spat sarcastically.

Tommy turned round and with one swift nod he stuck a beautiful Bolton handshake on Barry's smug, condescending dial.

Barry fell to the floor, Tommy grabbed him up and with one upper hook knocked him back down again!, picking him up one more time he dragged Barry to a large refuse container and knocked him smack bang inside it – he was covered in a week's slop of chicken livers, fish heads and rancid potato peel left over's.

'Get your own fucking uniform cleaned then while you're at it' he said.

The two Redcoats who were also accompanying us just stood there – I think they were secretly pleased – It needed to be done!

And so homeward bound!

GEORGIE

Three or Four months before we left for Pwhelli, I'd been having 'women problems' with my monthly cycle.

I'd been to the doctors several times and had tests done, even 2 pregnancy tests which showed negative.

I had weight loss, weight gain, back ache, nausea, felt like a bag of shit some days...couldn't understand what was wrong.

I started working in an office for a factory what gave gifts in exchange for vouchers that were collected in cigarette packets (no.6 and No.10 cigarettes).

 The factory was called No.6 and it was at the bottom of Stoneclough brow.

I'd been there a couple of months and had, had a particularly bad day, throwing up and feeling really ill.

This was Monday, I came home from work and arranged an appointment with my G.P – Doctor Gracie, who had a surgery in Mather Street, for the next day, after a check up he sent me for another pregnancy test.

In them days you peed in a empty tablet bottle and took it up to Townleys Hospital – then you had 2-3 days waiting for the results – there was no 'Clear Blue' home tests then..

Friday I rang the hospital – and was told my test had come back positive –

Shocked, Stunned, Happy, Sad, Frightened you name it I experienced every possible emotion.

Me and Tom had, had one of our regular fall-outs a couple of days before, so weren't speaking.

The first thing I did was ring my best buddy Nelly, and then Col, and we arranged to meet in the Market Inn next day – Saturday afternoon..

Never in a blue moon did I think I could of been pregnant, but it was what it was.

We'd been sat in the Market for over an hour when I got the urge to use the loo – and on doing so to my horror, I found I was losing blood, I was pretty street smart about most things in them days –

but this was completely new to me and I could only rely on my two buddies for help.

A weekend doctor was called and it was decided that I would be seen at a friend Linda's house not far away from the Market Inn – I hadn't even told my Mum yet so this was to save the hassle.

The lady doctor came and advised me to go home and keep my feet up off the ground – but to go directly to the hospital if the bleeding got worse.

I did this, and at the same time broke the news to my Mum, who was more shocked than me!

I rested in bed that night, but on getting up the next morning for the loo, I began to lose a lot more blood.

A family member took me up to the hospital, after all particulars had been taken I was given a bed on a ward and was told I hadn't to stand up or put my feet on the floor.

I lay there until the following morning using big grey ugly bed pans to pee in, and being checked every now and then by the ward nurse.

The next morning I was awakened by the nurse, who told me I was being examined by a doctor, and that they needed to check the baby's heartbeat, I was given an internal which in my condition was the most horrific thing I have ever had to tolerate, and then they checked for the heartbeat, yes they could hear it! ..

I was left then for several hours when I started getting really severe pains in my stomach – I called for the nurse and two more doctors came to my bedside again with their stethoscope, this time there was no heartbeat and I was asked to get out of bed and go into a side room where another doctor could examine me

– this I did – and endured yet another internal examination!

this I was then told to go back to my bed, I asked if i could use the adjoining loo, whilst I was up – they gave me another cardboard bed pan and told me to pee in it instead of down the toilet.

As I sat there on the loo I felt an enormous shooting pain across my stomach and at the base of my back and within seconds a small mound lay inside of the cardboard bed pan - I soon realised, naively or not - it was my baby.

I just stood there for what seemed like eternity, as reality dawned on me, in what i can only describe as fear and shock combined I began to scream and cry like I'd never stop.

A nurse run into the room, then ran back out to the doctor, who was a small Indian doctor in a sari, I can't or maybe don't want to remember her name, the nurse spoke to her then returned with some paper towels.

'Here take these' she said wrap the baby in them and go back to your bed, the doctor is just seeing another patient and will be with you as soon as she's finished'.

I honestly can't remember what was running through my mind at the time.

Completely numb I did what I was told, I sat there and waited holding the stillborn child.

I don't know how long I sat there holding the baby.

Eventually a nurse came and took him from me –

I was almost seven months pregnant and hadn't even realised – I'd only found out I was pregnant two days before this, and hadn't really got my head round it, all I did know was I felt an immense sense of sadness and loss and my tears were unstoppable.

I don't know how long it was after but my sister Pauline and my Mum were at the hospital, my other sister Kitty and her husband had gone to find Tom.

Later that evening I heard Tom's footsteps coming down the ward, he sat at the side of the bed saying nothing just holding my hand.

It was a huge shock to him too! Eventually we managed to talk and discuss just what we needed to discuss.

I was kept in hospital for another two days I had a D.C and waited for the doctor to discharge me.

I remember those last two nights lying there there still unable to take in the last few days events, I couldn't stop crying.

What I remember and will never forget was a lovely Nurse called Christine Bolton who spent those nights sat with me she really was an angel, and her kindness and compassion will always be remembered.

I also remember a friend walking up to my bed – Hilary, Marleys sister she hugged me and handed me a bag of fruit, telling me she was sorry.

It meant a lot, I needed a friendly face to help me get motivated and prepared to go home.

Days turned into weeks, weeks turned into months, I somehow managed to regulate myself to get back into normality.

My friends were brilliant offering support at all times.

Nights out became more regular, although I never could and never would forget 'Georgie' - that's what I would have christened my son if he had lived.

Even now I think about how he would have turned out, he would have been 42 years old now, Sherri-Lee would have been his little sister, and Jonathan his little brother.

Sadly fate still had some hands to deal me and in between giving birth to Sherri-lee and Jonathan, I lost 2 more children, and another child after Jonathan was born – all three were early pregnancies and were miscarriages, I learned to cope – but not to forget.

It was several years later when discussing this with a friend she told me that my daughter Sherri-Lee and my son Jonathan were both acknowledged as 'Rainbow' children....

She went on to explain that a child born after a still birth or a miscarriage was known as a 'Rainbow' child – She went on to explain that a 'Rainbow' appears after a storm - the storm refers to the loss of a child, and the 'Rainbow' appears after a storm with Sunshine – Sunshine being the birth of an healthy child. And I thank God I now have 2 healthy 'Rainbow' children

Me with my two lovely grown-up 'Rainbow' children Sherri-Lee & Jonathan (Although they have managed to throw in the occasional showers as they grew) .....and I'm still hoping for that 'pot of gold' to appear lol...

A HALF A LAGER , A BAG OF CRISPS...AND A BUNCH OF POPPIES?

Tommy lived hard and played hard, however, he treated me like a Princess most of the time (except when we argued and clashed horns and then he could be an awkward so and so)

He wasn't perfect and I suppose I turned a blind eye to some of his 'misgivings' but I knew he had good in him, our relationship which, after we had got married, and we had our children, blossomed into a trouble free family life.

His days of car 'borrowing', fighting and as a unrequested removal man for businesses and stores completely come to an halt.

We didn't have much money in them days (apart from the odd forgery – if you remember my story in Book 1)

One day, we went for a walk, up Highfield Road, it was a raging hot day and he bought 2 cans of lager from the local shop, and 2 bags of cheese &onion crisps.

We went round the back of the Flying Shuttle pub and sat in the large grass filled field at the back having our 'picnic' – and a cheeky snog!...

Out of the blue, Tommy got up and walked towards a large group of poppies that were growing nearby, he pulled at a bunch of them and came back and sat down

'Here these are for you' he said...'You know I love you more than anything in the world – and I know I always will – so will you marry me? '

The mouthful of lager I'd just drank sprayed all over Tommy, the poppies and into the open packets of crisps.

'Where the f*** did that just come from' I said...

'Well is that a Yes or a No?' he asked...I sat there and looked at the big soppy expression on his face ' Oh alright then' I said.

So romantic eh?...No Airship with 'will you marry me Alanah in the sky – No trip to the top of Eiffel Tower (even Blackpool tower would have scored him a couple of brownie points)

No Candlelit dinner and roses – but hey ho that's what happened.

And I can honestly say he more than made up for this throughout our marriage never once did he forget flowers, chocolates, dinner dates or Cards – on Birthday's Mothers Day or Valentines day -even if we'd had a row and weren't speaking ...Bloody good job eh ??

So that's how we decided to get hitched
In a nutshell, short and sweet!

And to this very day Poppies are still my
favourite flowers.

BWFC SKINS RULE O.K

The immortal words 'Skins Rule O.K' must have been sprayed, painted and daubed over every wall, bus shelter and toilet door in the late 70's.

I think there is one or two of these skinhead handiworks still knocking about today, what the graffiti police have missed.

One of the 'top' skins in Bolton at the time was a lad named Fred Dicky, a popular doorman, Lever Ender and generally known 'hard man'.

From what Ive been told Fred had ventured into 'enemy territory' - Walkden and Little Hulton, and he was approached and 'bovvered' by some of the natives there.

This didn't go down too well with the 'Bolton Lot' and a 'Hospitality Visit' was now on the cards.

(Or should that read 'Hospital Visit?').

Within a couple of days a battalion of skinheads were marching down Manny Road – 'Freds Barmy Army' and on their way the Farnworth lot joined the Bolton lot in unison.

– Fred was also a popular bloke in Farnworth.

So now just imagine a large assembly of rampant skinheads – there was easy 200 of them – And with regimental precision they manoeuvred their way to Walkden, like trained snipers cutting through side streets, derelict land and the black leach woodland area, so as not to raise suspicion from the 'dibble' on their way.

And like an all male parody of the 'Monteverdi Choir' they belted out their battle songs !

One of them being...

I'm a knock kneed chicken I'm a bow legged hen, I ain't been so happy since I don't know when, I walk when I wiggle and I wiggle when I walk, doing the 'BOLTON BOOT WALK'

- yep 200 guys – God only knows who made these 'never to be forgotten battle cries' up. But The Walkdeners and Little Hultoners had to be deaf not to hear it !

Approaching Walkden centre was like a scene from 'Saving Private Ryan' the towns were in battle, Shop windows were smashed, any lose metal object was snatched up and used along with lead piping, baseball bats, spanners, wrenches – anything that 'hurt' on contact

– Soon the cops arrived in their meat vans – jumping out truncheons in hands but scared shitless by the vast amount of skinheads involved.

I remember Topsy, Jimmy Kelly, Wally and few of the others surrounding one particular copper as he grabbed hold of one of our lads Glenn Roberts and tried to get him in the back of the police van –

 Glenn was a good six foot, weighed in at around 15 stone and unlike the rest of the lads – had a full head of shoulder length hair and a full 'garibaldi' beard –

and although to us he was a genuinely nice guy – he must have looked a proper 'bad ass' to the copper – however he eventually got him into the back of the van – which, has it drove off was bombarded with house bricks, rocks, metal bars, anything solid and available.

There was a lot of casualties that time, from the towns involved, but tomorrow was another day.

Apart from the occasional 'battles', Monday nights and Fridays in Walkden, was a bit of an hot spot for the Farnworth and Bolton Lot at Pembroke Halls civic Centre,

A Large dance floor, Live bands, a bar and great music...here the skins could compare their battle scars and check out the shine on their 'Docs' - and the girls could dance around their handbags and swap lip gloss – the good life!

ROCK 'N' ROLL DANCE

Pembroke Halls,
Worsley Road,
Walkden,
Worsley,
Manchester
Junction 13 off M63

Bank Holiday
Monday
28th May, 1984
2 pm to 12 pm

Tickets (advance) £5
(on the day) £6
From Paul Ramsbottom
6 Lord's Avenue, Weaste,
Salford M5 2HH
☎ 061-737 3924

CITY LIFE 21

A BLIGHTY'S TICKET FROM

NOEMBER 1972

FAMILIES

There were several families in Farnworth, some stood out more than most, brothers and sisters who were protective, loyal, and stayed together no matter what life threw at them..

The Longworths were one of these families brought up by their lovely Mum Brenda, The lads Alan, Ian, Paul and Mick were long time friends of my husband Tom, knew him before I did,

 They were 'proper lads' no fear of anyone – except of their Mum Brenda who knew when to pull the reins when needed – and I'm sure there were several occasions when she had to lol...

Then there was Julie, Joanne, and twin brother Dave, who passed away some years ago, but has never been forgotten by his family.

One thing about the Longworths, If one of the family broke their leg – they all limped.

Two of the Longworth brothers, Ian & Mick

The Magaris were another sturdy family, alsowith a strong Mother Philemina, a lovelylady small and petite, with a strong Italian smile.

I have a special memory of the lovely Philemina, from when I gave birth to my daughter Sherri-Lee, in Townleys hospital, I'd had a particularly difficult birth, 36 hours of sheer agony lol... and Sherri-Lee was a 'breach' baby which meant her bottom come out first.

I remember the midwife saying, 'She's being awkward coming out the wrong way!....

Today, I still think to myself – She's not changed much !! she's still bloody awkward now!! After 40 years.

Philemina was the first face I saw, when I woke up – She placed a large plate of ham & tongue salad sandwiches on my side table what she had made especially for me – she worked in the kitchen at the hospital.

Them butties went down a treat - and were the best butties I've ever tasted.

I went to school with the Magari's Emmanuel (Maggi) was in my class – and he would keep the class amused in our History lesson with his buddy, Ste Whittlestone' –

They would show some amazing skills with a Manchester United scarf.....much to the annoyance of our teacher Jack Walsh who could never understand why or what the class was always in fits of giggles about!

But I daren't say what it was in my book lol...

Then there was Pete, Rocco, Louis, Vic,

Maria and Marguerita, sadly Louis
passed away a couple of years ago. But
the family is still going strong!...

I could tell some tales about them – but
not in this book lol !

Rocco Magari & Mum Philemina

Louis & Emmanuel (Maggi) Magari

Louis, Vic, Philemina, Pete & Maria
Magari

GRAHAM & GRAHAM

Although me, Nelly and Col were dating
Tom, Brad and Dave, we often argued
and fell out with them for a few days
sometimes a week!

Usually we tried to make sure we could
manage a triple 3-4 day break-up with
them at the same time, so us three
could have a few girly nights of hitting
the town and having a few cheeky
snogs with one or two other lads without
a guilt trip !

The night we all went on Debs hen party
was one of these nights.   There was
loads of us, Me, Nelly, Col, Debs (of
course or else it would be pointless or
maybe not lol)

Bev Wilky, Maxine Hunt, Karen Rimmer,

Susan Thornbourough, Sue Boothsman,

Helen Pollitt, Viv Walsh, Val Rigby,

Brenda Berry, Julie Arrowsmith, Denise Barlow, Pauline Burke, Kath Alker, Angela Smith,Maggie Dunbarton (Bessel) , Anita Hunt, and on, and on and on...

We'd booked a coach to take us to the Bier Keller at Belle Vue in Manchester,

Halfway through the night me and Col had met these two blokes, both called 'Graham' they were rugby players for either 'Wigan' or St.Helen's – can't remember which.

I took a shine to Blonde Graham, because I thought he looked identical to'David Soul', a popular actor at that time in a hit series called 'Starsky & Hutch'.

 And at the end of the night we drunkenly gave them a phone number to contact us – It's surprising how a few steins of Stella or Heniken can make you throw all caution to the wind!!

But none the less we've all been there at some time - I'm sure...anyway getting on our coach back...

We said our goodbyes and thought nothingof it.

Debs the 'bride to be' was completely leathered and she had, unknown to us sneaked this guy from Cheshire onto our coach – poor lad – hadn't a clue what had hit him – one lad on a coach of 24 pissed up relentless vixens.

He managed to survive theordeal and joined about 12 of us back in Farnworth at Debs house which was also an......off license. – well at least we knew PG

Tips wasn't on the breakfast menu!

What we didn't know was – Deb's husband to be's' stag party had also decided to crash at the off-license too, and our respective boyfriends were also there, Tom, Bren, Dave,Plus Eeky, Robbie, Wrighty, Mick, Brian etc..

They took one look at the lad from Cheshire getting off the coach, and each one of them decided it was one of us who had brought him back.

The Cheshire lad was chased all the way down Longcauseway at 3 am, by

our blustering bloodhound boyfriends.

I haven't a clue how this poor lad got home, but I bet he thought twice before hitching a mystery ride with anyone again for a long time!

The lads returned and all hell broke loose, It was like a scene from last of the Mohicans we each got blamed individually for being with this lad None of us could say it was Debs (we couldn't rock the boat she was Getting married in a week).

I remember me and Tom arguing, upstairs in the bathroom going at it hammer and tongue, then one of our girls Bev Wilky come running up the stairs and in a drunken frenzy.

She jumped onto Tommy's back, 'It wasn't Alanah who brought him back' she yelled as she clutched tight onto his back, arms tightly gripping his neck, riding Tommy like a professional Texas rodeo star. – you go girl !

Well eventually all became calm, and tomorrow rolled on..

That week, Debs owned up, telling the lads it was her that had brought the Cheshire lad onto the coach, as a favour to him as he needed a lift back towards Bolton as he had missed his coach from the Bier Keller.

(Yes it was a lie – but a believable one).

Tommy, Brad and Dave spent all the week trying to make up to us for their 'wrongful' accusations – well to some extent anyway.

We made them suffer, I got a new pair of Derbas heels, Col got a new top and Nelly got a Jacket.

I think we were all wearing these on the Saturday night we went to meet our lads in the Market....Not a care in the world...until we pulled aside the red velvet curtain that covered the entrance to the lounge....

Sat right bang facing us was

....Graham & Graham !!...Never in my life have I felt such a surge of sheer panic, Col turned white, Nelly turned green!..

'Hi girls – big surprise' said raham...Yes one big Fuck Off surprise !!..

It seems that on that drunken night in Manchester the telephone number we had given them was for the Market Inn.

They had apparently rang several times over the last week and decided to come pay us a visit – In a mad frenzy with legs like two watered down trifles we somehow managed to get the 'Grahams' to change venue –

pretty bloody quick before the 'Bowery' boys came a knockin!! ....what a nightmare!...We – me and Col ended up taking them to the Top Club (Farnworth Labour club) a place we knew was safe from prying eyes and Tom and Dave.

Lying wasn't a problem - lying was our second nature we managed to convince the 'Grahams' that we were leaving the following Monday – to go and live and working the U.S.A as assistants to producers for.........

Tamla Motown ....

Oh My.. the lies just rolled from our tongues, we blagged every question they threw at us ...but hey ho they were suitably convinced and with good luck gestures and a chicken in the basket supper we said our goodbyes....

That was a bloody close shave...Tom or Dave were never the wiser.

We got back to the Market Inn about 10.30 p.m

And, explained our earlier absence to Tom and Dave, saying that Cols mum had been trapped in a deck chair and we had to go up to the hospital with her for a check up.

The things us women have to do just to keep the peace eh ??

Me, Nelly, Col and Pauline still great buddies after 40 odd years..

'The Original Golden Girls' lolol

TV MEMORIES

Think we all had one or two of our own

favourite T.V shows in the 70's and 80's.

I remember in the late 60's we got our first colour T.V, a 'Decca' it was in a large teak cabinet with concertina style draw to doors.

My Mum would polish it every morning, reminding my Dad 'We didn't get it given us – stop putting your finger marks on it'

There were loads of good programmes to watch, a lot better than todays rubbish..

So I'll start off with a few of the kiddies shows

They don't make em now like they use to do....

Andy Pandy, Teddy and Louby Lou. Picture

Book. Rag, Tag & Bobtail. Tales of the

Riverbank.   Bill & Ben (not forgetting 'little weed').

Wooden Tops with Spotty the dog.

Four Feather Falls (remember the magic guns of Tex Tucker).

Fireball XL5 and Colonel Steve Zodiac, Robert the Robot and Zoonie the Lazoon – pet of Dr.Venus.

Pipkins with Hartley the Hare, Pig and Topov.

Tiswas, Bagpuss, Play School, Magic Roundabout. The Littlest Hobo (I loved that dog).

Bananaman. Cockleshell Bay.

Black Beauty. Lightening Tree.

Petticoat Junction with Billy Jo, Bobby Jo and Betty Jo.

Gilligans island (I'll never forget the theme tune to this).

Beverley Hill Billy's (granny would have sorted out Farnworth not rights lol).

Happy Days. Different Strokes (What

you talking about Arnold??). Mork & Mindy (Nanoo Nanoo).

The Jetsons with George, Elroy, Jane and Judy and their flying car.

The Love Boat. Fantasy Island (The Plane –The plane).

Knight Rider (David Hasseldorf)artificial intelligence was never as cool as Kitt, his souped up Trans Am.

Alf (an alien named Gordon Shumway) who crash lands in the Tanners backyard.

TheTwighlight Zone – I remember buying packs of swap cards with pictures of the aliens on when I was at school (St.Gregory's) I had a big wedge of cards and Mr Greenhalgh (Ganger) the headmaster confiscated them all because I was swapping them in morning assembly.

Married with Children was a traditional

family sitcom with Al Bundy and his wife

Peggy, it was controversial at the time – and also very funny.

Dallas (did we ever find out who really shot J.R or were we dreaming lol).

 3-2-1 with Dusty bin and his wingman Ted Rogers. I still can't get my fingers round doing it.

M.A.S.H. Alias Smith & Jones. Kung Fu. George & Mildred. On the Buses. Follyfoot. Love Thy Neighbour. Mrs Thursday. Dukes of Hazzard. Starsky & Hutch.

The Golden Girls – a title me, Nelly and Col have acquired over the last something years lol .

Never mind the quality feel the width.

My Favourite Martian. Mr Ed. Talking horse.

The Man From U.N.C.L.E –(United Network Command for Law and Enforcement) Napoleon Solo and Iiilya Kuryakin –

My Mum bought me a toy spy set from this show from the Papershop in Glynne Street, I really thought I was spy !! and would hide in the garages at the top of back street, with my plastic gun and spy note pad – Till one day...

David Whittle (Pollywick) came and broke my gun and nicked my badge !!!

I won't go on any further with T.V shows I'm sure there's hundreds I've forgot, but what I will do is mention 2 or 3 or maybe 4 games

we used to play as kids - just for good

measure and to add an extra page of text to my book !

I remember playing 'Elastics' in the school yard – we'd use about 5 yards of elastic tied together end to end then two of us would hook it around our ankles with feet apart, then a third person would jump into centre and make different shapes with their feet using the elastic as the source – I can't explain it any better than that but I'm sure most of you know what I'm talking about.

Then there was 'The Farmer wants a wife' .. A large group of us would make a circle holding hands and one person (the farmer) would stand in the middle we'd all walk round till he picked one of us to be his or even her wife, then it carried on with a baby, a nurse, a dog a bone etc etc..there was always someone left in the circle who created a stink because they weren't picked.

Klackers – yep that's what they were called – appropriately it seems as they were two hard plastic golf sized balls each tied to a length of string (about 6 inches) we'd then raise our hand holding them and move it rigorously up and down till they – 'Klacked' together.

Yep proper boring ! that's probably why you'd see most of them slung high up tangled amongst telephone cables or lamp posts.

Tin Can Stompers....these highly inventative kids amusers were made up of 2 tin cans, usually Mums, batchelor peas or Beinz Meinz Heinz tins – emptied and usually cleaned out then two holes made at the top of each can and a long length of string was threaded, hooped then tied, we'd then stand on the tins holding the string forbalance and .....stomp!! ......beats the ipad hands down...well that's what the kids these days are told...it's not even debatable is it

I can't even begin to compare the good old

70's & 80's game of 'British Bulldog' with

today's Segways-Hoverboards......lolol

so I won't.....

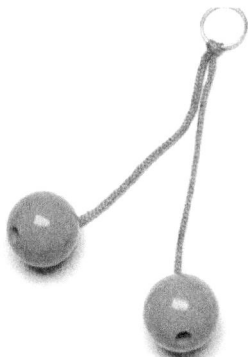

Klacker's – looks more like something you'd buy from an Anne Summers party ! – rather than a kids toy !

Man from U.N.C.L.E spy set, who had one of these ?

And David (Pollywick) Whittle if you read this ! I want my gun and badge back !

Remembers these classics ?

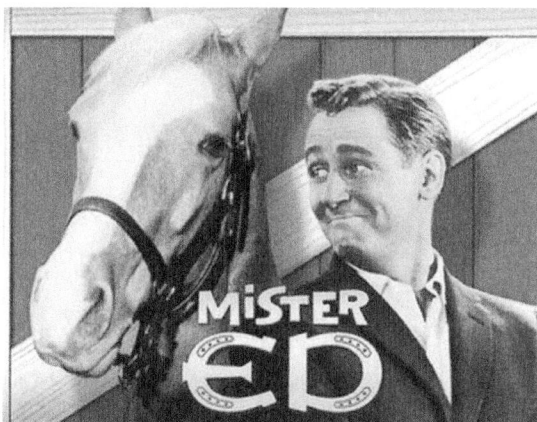

ELVIS

The 'Big Apple' was one of the main
social hubs of the Farnworth crew it later
became 'Troggs' in the later end of the
80's..

Here was a meeting place for the skins
to discuss battles, battle tactics, music
and who was the best 'speed' dealer
etc..

The lads would check out one anothers
'Ben Shermans', 'Farrahs' and 'Royals'
– and check out the skinhead girls in
pecking order.

There was a great bond of loyalty
between them all – although some of
the lads would occasionally take the
piss out of each other for a laugh...

 And one particular lad comes

to mind...

To save embarrassment I'm not going to

mention the real name of this guy, enough said he was one of the Farnworth lot' he loved Elvis Presley with a passion and so I'll call him Elvis.

Now Elvis was a 16 stone, 6 foot four grizzly bear of a fella.

To the untrained eye..he was a force to be reckoned with – but to us Farnworth lot he was a 'pussy' ... Elvis was as soft as a box of Andrex tissues.

Not an ounce of malice or harm in him – and definitely gullible – an endearing 'ForestGump' in other words - an easy target...

The lads used to have a field day with him.

One particular night in the 'Apple', Elvis,after way too many snakebites fell asleep on a corner table –

 It wasn't too long before the lads clocked him.

John Unsworth and Davis hovered over like two blue horse fly's and with a few swift swipes of a 'BIC' razor, shaved both of his large black bushy eye brows clean off...

everyone was doubled over crying with laughter. When Elvis was woken up at closing time he doddered home still oblivious at what had happened.

The next night in the 'Apple' most of us waited in anticipation for Elvis to make an appearance.

10.30 the doors swung open in walked eyebrow less Elvis, face like a raging wildebeest 'You fucking bastards – the lot of you!!' he yelled

the music stopped and within a couple of seconds – the entire room was shaking with proper belly laughter

– Elvis kept a straight face through it all,

'You O.K Elvis ?' said Mick Hughes
'You're not looking yourself tonight
mate'...more belly laughs..

'Something different about you Elvis –
something missing' said John McMahon
(Maccy).. '

Yeh think something on your face
playing hide and seek with you!' said
Wally.

by now everyone throwing comments to
the stone faced Elvis and getting more
and more giddy with every comment

...then the D.J started the music

......'SEXY EYES' by Dr.Hook & the
MedicineShow..

followed by 'DOCTOR MY EYES' bythe
Jacksons ..

finishing off with 'BRIGHT EYES' BY
Art Garfunkel...

everyone went absolutely mental –
except Elvis who kept a straight face
throughout the remainder of the night.

 (Thinking about his face, now it reminds
me of 'Boysie' in 'Only Fools and Horses
after he'd been conned by Delboy and
Rodney!)

Trouble was ..the more serious Elvis's
face got ..the more Uncontrollable we
all got, we laughed until our sides hurt.

Don't think anyone of us has ever
laughed like we did that night...our filters
disappeared – just like Elvis's eye
brows..

But the tomfoolery didn't stop there,
poor Elvis was now flavour of the month
for the lads... there was more yet to
come..

RUMBELOWS

For a while, about 12 months in between Horwich College and G.U.S I worked at Rumbelows head office on ManchesterRoad, a decent job in the meters office, with my long time buddy Val.

our bosses wereJoe 'Sherlock' and Brian 'Holmes' lol weird ?

Anyhow me and Val were the P.A's for these guys and enjoyed fabulous lunches in Town taking minutes at meetings. Life was great!

However, as in most offices there's always a nob head, one you just DONT get on with, who pisses you off just by breathing – well Morris Shufflebottom was this particular nob head – (that wasn't his real last name I just thought it sounded good!)

now I'm writing this down I feel really harsh and cruel – OK , maybe not ! lol

Morris was the office ass licker, grass and wannabe, he scuttled around the desks like a sewer rat scavenging for any gossip, errors, or banned cups of coffee we might have sneaked in when Joe Sherlock or Brian Holmes weren't looking.

Me and Val took it upon ourselves on behalf of other staff members that Morris had annoyed – to ensure he was kept occupied at all times!

It started off with filling his desk drawers (obviously when he wasn't there) with the Christmas decorations we had pulled down in January – this was now March, he looked a little bewildered when he opened his drawer but said nothing! – no effect.

so our next step was to change all the letters around on his office keyboard, it took him most of the morning to re-arrange them all back into order – and he wasn't too happy lol...

We'd now acquired a taste for revenge on Morris.

Our next step was going in work early one morning and with the help of one or two other staff members we moved Morris's desk and all his equipment to a solitary space right at the back of the office and painted his cream office phone with flowers and butterflies with white copydex and black marker.

Morris came into work – first of all he was confused as to where his desk had gone?, seeing all the staff then with their faces red and ready for bursting into laughter – his beady eyes scoured the large room till he saw his desk – marching over he noticed straight away the pretty flower and butterfly detail we had chosen for him, he was furious and frog marched himself into Joe Sherlocks office to complain.

Joe Sherlock was a great boss, and I think, Morris could piss him off too at times,

However he was the boss and after trying to find the actual culprits unsuccessfully, we all got away with a 'warning'.

Now , in our office canteen/dining room we had a large fridge which we could use to store our lunch – in sandwich boxes with our names wrote on them.

Every day without fail Morris would bring his clear blue lidded tupper-ware box – always the same 'Tuna & Mayo wholemeal butties, and a can of Tizer

This day however we decided to scrape the tuna from the bread and replace it with a smearing of 'Kit-E-Kat' cat food we had in for our office moggie 'Cleo'...

The canteen was busier than usual that lunch time – word had spread lol..

Morris sat there as usual, and opened his lunchbox, the atmosphere was eerily quiet – but buzzing with electric anticipation of that first bite he would take.

Everyone's eyes avoiding contact with
Morris as he did so...

Now believe it or not, that poor lad
finished every last crumb of them
sandwiches – without a murmur, only
stopping for mouthfuls of his Tizer...

on finishing he then returned back to his
office desk,.

well I can only say the atmosphere in
that room the whole afternoon was one
of the funniest days I've ever spent
working.

not that much work was done that day,
everyone was too busy making cat
noises when they passed Morris,singing
'Pussy cat Pussy cat by Tom Jones and
generally referring any 'Cat' related
word associations with their
conversation to him – such as 'Hey
Morris – can I borrow your CATalogue',
Hey Morris which CATegory does these
files go in?' even to the point of silliness
when someone asked did he like tomato
Catchup on his chips..

.Morris never caught on though...

The final straw came when we found a pile of his business cards on his desk and at the top of the cards.

In bold print was Rumbelows Head Office, his name and telephone number and his job status which was 'General office clerk' –

It took us a couple of days but we managed to get the printing office of our company to duplicate them except change the title of 'General office clerk' to 'General sausage puller'

he passed them business cards to everyone he met – never once realising the alteration on them.

It was when one of our Big Managers called in at the office and Morris passed one on to him...

.All hell broke loose – this time Morris made an official complaint, it resulted in me and Val getting a written warning –

but believe me the fun we had.... it was
bloody well worth it ...

Morris didn't stay working there long
after that, we heard he'd found another
job – at Walls in the office as an invoice
clerk for cooked meats – and sausages
lolol....

ON MOTHER KELLYS DOORSTEP – DOWN PALATINE ROAD

One night the Farnworth lads were in the 'Apple' arranging a night at the Mecca in Blackpool.

some of the older lads would sometimes pay a visit to a B & B near Palatine Road, at the time known as a 'Brasshouse'

Mrs Kelly who ran it with a rod of steel, would make sure their special requirements for the night were fulfilled to the full if she could.

It was arranged that 3 or 4 of the lads would go on the Friday night before the Mecca club on the Saturday, they were on a mission to help 'Elvis' lose his virginity, he'd never even had a girlfriend let alone anything else, they reached the B & B and explained the situation to Mrs K...and then some –

these lads were relentless.

Meeting up with the rest of the crew inBlackpool the following night.

They finally persuaded 'Elvis' – that 'It washis time to become a man'.

Elvis after his refusals were heard on deaf ears, finally agreed nervously.

Mrs Kelly, was ready and waiting to eventually award Elvis his 'V' badge.

with a quick wink of the eye from one of the lads Mrs Kelly ushered Elvis into one of the Dingy bedrooms and told him to prepare himself to 'capture the flag!' and she left.

Minutes later she returned and ushered one of her 'speciality' girls, hand chosen by the lads.

Her name was 'Bridget' her 'house' name was 'Bridget the Midget' – I can only imagine the look on Elvis's face when she entered the room.

Elvis stood 6 foot four in his stocking feet – and Bridget just topped the tape at 4 foot three, the lads laughter could be heard at Cleveleys.

Sadly Elvis never managed to earn his badge , – but the lads insisted it was well worth the twenty quid just for the memory of it!

A couple of years later Elvis met his perfect match, married her and moved to Brighton.

I Don't think for one minute he will ever forget that night! – hopefully now though, if he does remember it will be with a big grin

on his face!

SLOW POKE

Slow poke was a legend to himself, he lived in a derelict caravan somewhere on the way heading towards Salford.

he would be describe nowadays as an hermit, we just considered him a homeless loser in life.

We heard he was estranged from his family, his Mother and a sister, and for some unknown reason had not spoke to them for years.

Slow Poke was dirty, grubby and smelly, but strangely we didn't mind him sitting on the 'warry' with us on sunny days, where he would strum, his only prized possession – his guitar, and boy could he play that thing.

He told us the guitar was signed for him by an American musician 'Muddy Waters' who was known as the Father of the modern Chicago blues.

Slow Poke would sometimes share a spliff with us...Some of us would buy him a pasty from Birches pasty shop,

and he'd wash it down with a bottle of 'barley wine' which he always had in his weatherworn jacket pocket.

Slow Poke seemed a 'sad' loner he gave the impression he had, had a very hard life, his weathered face worn and wrinkled was probably portraying his age at least 30 years older than what he was.

he was harmless though and never judged anyone of us.

One dark night walking on his way home, he was attacked by a couple of lads near Swinton, he wouldn't of stood a chance in defending himself, he was six stone pissed wet through, he was beaten to a pulp and left badly bruised, broken and bleeding at the roadside.

A resident called the ambulance, and he was taken to the hospital, some of us went to visit, Police were involved, but he could offer no information as to who had done it or why

and so, no charges were ever made.

Also his prized guitar had also gone missing.

After he was discharged from the hospital, Slow Poke never ventured far from his caravan from then on.

Months went by and one night down at the Wishing Well, club in Swinton, our lads got talking to some of the 'Swintoners' and were told about of a couple of deadbeat crackheads who had been bragging about beating this old guy up and nicking his guitar.

more information was given and our lads came back to the Market Inn with 2 names.

A couple of nights later Tommy, Mick, Brad, Eeky and Robbie went back down to Swinton, 'geared up' and to 'make it right'for Slow Poke...

From the tales told after (and I know a tale always gets exaggerated) the two lads had both been frog marched to their flat and the guitar was retrieved, (still with the signature of 'Muddy Waters' intact).

The lads got their just desserts, both got a good hiding, as our lads 'doc martens'

played tribute to their generals and two colonels – or has Robbie crudely put it 'They got their bald Headed yoghurt slingers smashed' ....sorry ..but that's what he said!

And a few days later we all paid a visit to Slow Poke and the look in his eyes when he saw the guitar ...was ...yes.....priceless.

Slow Poke passed away several months later....

– he's up in 'guitar strummers heaven –

now 'jamming' with his pal

.......Muddy waters..

NOT RIGHTS, EYE SIGHTS AND ARSE WIPES

This next chapter is exactly about what it says in the title, Only difference being the names are made up – but the characters are 100% real.

this saves a lot of confrontation whenever I'm out in the street, and also a way of making sure to keep my bodyintact, unbroken, and with no black eyes.

I've tried to describe them all accurately and 'truthfully' as I can – I'm sure you will be able to relate to some of the characters in some way – We've all got one in our street!

And I'm definitely no exception to the rule – after being neighbours to a 'cloned' Fred and Rose West for several years....

Wyndike Winnie

Wideload Winnie Wyndike, was a regular in Farnworth centre, she must of weighed in at 20 stones.

She had a big round head, with two small black beady eyes, that looked like tiny piss holes in the snow.

Short unkempt hair and a passion for pies and pasties in large quantities, no matter when or where you saw her – she always had a 'Peter Hunts' in her inflated paws.

Her red bulging, jaws always chomping away, she wore a checked cheesecloth shirt 3 sizes too small that fastened up the front – exposing her manky grey bra and unruly boobs in between the stretched to the max gaps of the buttonholes, and a pair of black stretchy'crimpolene' bell bottomed pants.

Believe me if she sat on a chair – she could visit two towns at the same time!..

Her little 2 year old kid would always be sat in his 'mamas & papas' buggy, watching every mouthful she took, and waiting eagerly for a piece of pie crust she would offer him every now and again.

Her boyfriend One tooth Tony, weighed in at about 6 stone and was the length of a lamp post.

Now before anyone jumps on the bandwagon and accuses me of disrespecting 'overweight' people, I realise not every over weight person is responsible for being obese , there are many reasons, Thyroid glands, Psychological disorders,Genetics, and Medication etc..

I too have had my share of over enthusiastic wobbly bits and unwelcome body fat – in excess!

But Wyndike Winnie was a 'Fat, lazy, greedy human waste consumption unit, and in my eyes didn't deserve any excuses made for the state she had solely created for herself !

One Pull Pete

There's a couple of reasons for his title of 'One Pull Pete' – the first one you're going to have to use your imagination,

I'm sure you will eventually clock on as to what that is!

The second reason being that Pete was always out on 'the pull' he had no filter or preferences – a 'hit' was an 'hit' in his books, unfortunately Pete didn't achieve many 'hits' but if you could win a prize for 'persistence' Pete would have his shelf full.

With his Jet black hair 'brylcreemed' back and dark slitty eyes, crooked teeth, he'd admire himself in the mirror – obviously a victim of a reality disorder.

Weekends he'd scuttle round take a shower, shave, supply of breath fresheners (or polo mints) in his top pocket and an abundance of 'Hi Karate' or 'Old Spice' aftershave poured around every crevice of his body.

Then slipping on his 'Dad & Lads'
anorak he Would letch around the
pubs, looking for single and hopefully
'naive' unaware prey.

His hands would slither across the
shoulders of 'Halter neck' dress or vest
top wearing girls as he passed 'Excuse
me girls' he'd say as he pretended to
squeeze past.

He weren't fucking going anywhere –
just backwards and forwards most of the
night! What a pillock !

Dirty Daz & Sticky Vicky

Ahh ! – a match made in heaven, Daz & Vicky...

Lived together on the local estate with their 5 kids in a two bed roomed council house.

Daz had a job, working nights – he was a burglar !

Each night he don his work clothes, black pants, black jumper, Nike trainers and black balaclava and off he went scouring the neighbourhood gardens for unlocked or easy to unlock garden sheds.

He was paid by the hour depending on how many bikes or lawnmowers he could collect per household.

Sometimes he would make a bonus by lifting a Bosch, Black & Decker or Makita treasured family Power tool.

All would be sold on to anyone who had no morals!! –

and there were plenty with the attitude 'Well if I don't buy it – Someone else will!'

Sticky Vicky – She would spend her days like a human sloth, if she wasn't screaming at the kids or smoking weed she would be making a big effort of doing 'Fuck All!' –

There was always some 'no mark' willing to sit with her sharing the ambience of being a dead leg, drinking typhoo from dirty mugs and rummaging down side of the couch for filter tips for her golden Virginia roll-ups.

'Sticky' only needed to leave her house when she went clothes shopping for herself and her kids – a what a talent she had – for whipping the clothes from the washing lines of neighbouring houses –

she would be in and out of them
gardens faster than a rocket full of
monkeys!

Yukan Pullitoffski

Yukan was from Poland and the original Jack of All Trades and local 'supplier' of Garden & Household items - Yukon could peel an orange in his pocket !

His ability to dismantle most 'available' structures in the fastest possible time (usually from more privileged areas when no-one was looking) e.g; Garden Furniture Children's Swings, Hanging Baskets, Large 'gas' barbeques, Garden decorations and tubs (even a small garden shed with all its contents on one occasion) was a talent not to be ignored

– His shoplifting skills also became renown Locally, and he would often amass lists from hopeful buyers (usually at Christmas time) for his loot !

He could, without any great effort shoplift the 'unshopliftable'. – microwaves, Pressure cookers, Video recorders, Pan sets, Cassette Players, Lamps, Irons – anything you might

find in an Argos catalogue today,
anything that was light enough to carry –
Yukan was your man!

Strangely enough, he was quite a
'likeable' person, and even stranger he
was accepted by a lot the community,
he wasn't one of the 'rough' ones.

I heard he'd even given some items to
some families who genuinely needed
stuff but couldn't afford to pay.

– A 'kindness' of sorts I suppose.

Yukon eventually met his wife, a school
headmistress from a neighbouring town,
and settled down.

I saw him in Farnworth a couple of years
ago, he was on his way to Asda....

Let's hope he remembered to take his
wallet with him..

Big Ben

Big Ben – wasn't a 'chimer' he was a 'charmer', and he was in fact just over 4 foot 6 tall, and one of the bonniest lads I ever knew'

Shaved head, big bright blue 'goo goo' eyes embellished with thick black eyelashes, and the cheekiest of all smiles.

His older brother was the complete opposite, six foot 2 and a face like a pit bulls anus.

Ben lived somewhere up Halliwell, but had a few mates in Farnworth and would 'drop in' to the Market Inn for a pint occasionally.

A Cracking Northern Soul dancer and a regular traveller to 'The Torch' soul club in Stoke.

I remember going to the 'Va Va all

nighter once in Bolton, there was a bit of

a fracas between a couple of Bolton lads and a few Chorley lads, Big Ben, dived in uninvited, hard as a bag of Blackpool Rock that lad.

He hadn't a clue what the 'bovver' was, he just joined in.

The Bouncers threw all the lads out – except for Ben – they couldn't see him hiding behind the 6 foot structures of Col & Phil Aloemi and a chunky Lester Roach.

Size was never an issue for Ben and he always managed to 'cop off' with one of the 'nights' prettiest skin girls.

His charm and his banter exceeded any height barrier.

Fanlight Fanny & Lucy lastic

If these two ever went out on a Saturday night without managing some 'Rocking &Cocking' on an empty stall on Farnworth Market on their way home in the early hours....

– then it would have been a complete waste of time them going out without their knickers on in the first place !

Fanny was an un-relentless trollop hard faced and scruffy, face covered in spots and scabs created by layers of un washed pan stick make-up, Laddered tights, greasy oily thick black hair -(and that was just under her arm pits!)

She was a moose - both she and Lucy enjoyed any attention they could get from the 'after hours' drinkers as they rolled out the pubs.

Once or twice they had attempted to invade 'The Big Apple' but were soon offered options of either leaving or being smacked round the head by about 20 'Chelsea Girl' handbags on orders from resident 'hard' girl Linda Battle (and that really was her name – and nobody had a surname that fitted as

perfect to her persona as hers did).

Linda didn't give a toss about anything or anybody she was as hard as the hobs of hell.

Old pals – Billy's book signing 'Dead Man Running at theChurch Hotel

Roy Ish, Tony Cunliffe, Baz Hindley, Max, Stan Berry, Billy, Joey Dean, Me, Brooky, Topsy, Gilly asnd Bodge

Max on a 'home visit from Oz with pals
Bev Wilky & Paul Topping (Topsy)

Towny and Pablo – 'Undressed' lol

Marley (Harvey), Me, Nelly, Tommy B, and Brad (Bren) this was taken in Newquay when we all went to pay our last respects to our

Beer Festival Britt – Max, Kath Alker (Robinson) & Me

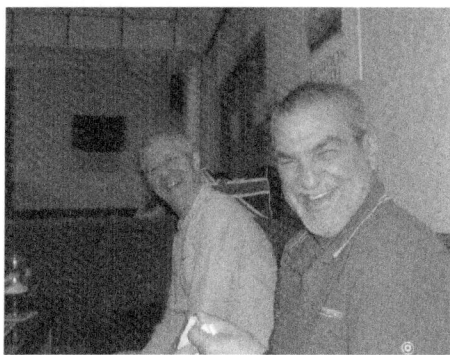

Bernie Pearson – and 'old blue eyes'
Gaz Roscoe - ' Soul Night' in Black
Horse

Pete and Murphy – Pete bought Murphy
a zimmer frame for his 60th Birthday,
took him 3 hours to wrap it up - lol

David Heathcote (Eeky) – a voice
louder than a foghorn – I don't think he
had one single enemy R.I.P my buddy

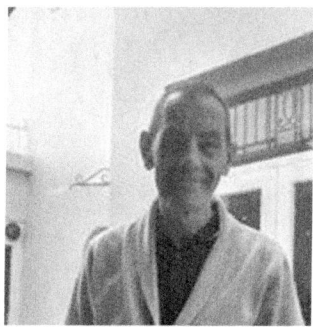

Dave (Pollywick) Whittle

My Man from U.N.C.L.E Sabateur

Jack & Karen Cartwright – If you read
Book 1 it's THE 'Jack'

Micky & Elaine Waters – much
respected Landlord & Landlady of the
'Blackhorse' and also a long time friend

My pal Debra Booth (Debs) Her B & B
was the best she lived in an off license

Hilary Clugstone one of 'the girls' and
Harveys sister

Chris 'Bandana man' Shaw one of the
Shaw brothers

Julie (Walsham) Robinson, First farny
girl to get her 'Harrington' Jacket
(Burgundy –if my memory serves me)
GRRRR ! me and Nell thought we were
!...lol

Barry (Baz) Seddon – 'Farny lad' and
brilliant dancer!

Karen Rimmer another 'Farny girl' and
friend

Fred 'Dicky' long time friend and well
respected Boltonian – original Burnden
Bovver Boy, Top Doorman and proud
Northern soul man

'Scouse' (on the left) another long time
friend and Boltonian doorman

Dave Howard one of the Farnworth crew

Maggie Dunbarton (Bessell) Still a
'Farny girl'

Jimmy Kelly's Birthday bash – brilliant night (Fancy dress 60's)

Jack Cartwright, Brian Howarth, Jimmy 'Birthday boy' Kelly, Billy Ish, Tony, and Stan Berry

Mick Walsh (Wally) one of the 'Saddle' lot

Roy Isherwood – Billy's little bro

John McMahon (Maccy)and his lovely wife Anne

Pablo, Glenn 'Moonshine' Roberts & Dave Buckley

Tommy 'B' & Jimmy Murphy on Tom's
60th Birthday celebration in St.Gregory's
club

THE FINAL 'FINAL' CHAPTER

I've noticed that a Lot of people who write books like to dedicate it to someone special in their lives.....

Well in 60 odd years I've met lots of people who I've loved and who held a special place in my heart (and still do) sadly a lot have passed to The 'Big Castle in the sky' – and some have passed in the opposite direction and will be toasting crumpets and marshmallows on the fire...but I'll never forget them or the years we all shared...so

here we go....

First of all My Mr Magoo Tommy Belk – who shared with me 45 years of his life,

My beautiful, kind hearted sister Kathleen Unsworth (Kitty),

 My Nephew Mark Ramsden Taken far too soon,... and his Dad my Brother (in-law) Michael Ramsden a character in his own right,

My Brother (in-law) Roy Unsworth.

My Thorn in the side and great friend, David Heathcote (Eeky) - if he managed to get into heaven, the angels will definitely be wearing ear plugs!.

Mick and Les Robinson, Mick Bulliss, Dave Jolly, Paul Sutty, Linda Battle, Judith Fulford (Brighteyes),

 Glen Worthington, Stephen Lane, John Gilbert (Gilly).

R.I.P my lovely family & friends ...until we meet again....................

Im sure that somewhere along the line you will have memories of your own family and friends who may be gone but not forgotten so I have left the following pages blank..

Maybe you would like to write your own down in memory of them....

199

Once again, many thanks for taking the time to read my books...

Alanah Belk xx

Printed in Great Britain
by Amazon